I CAN READ ABOUT

CATS AND KITTENS

Written by George Wolff

Illustrated by Barbara Kent

Troll Associates

Many people like cats and kittens
for their soft fur and beautiful eyes.

A cat's grace and strength sometimes remind us of powerful big cats like tigers.

Lions, tigers, and pet cats are all closely related. They all belong to the cat family.

PUMA

BOBCAT

Some cats purr, while other cats roar. The house cat purrs. Wild cats like the puma, lynx, bobcat and ocelot also purr.

HOUSE CAT

LYNX

OCELOT

LION

TIGER

LEOPARD

But lions, tigers, leopards, jaguars and cheetahs all roar.

CHEETAH

JAGUAR

Cats are meat eaters. A house cat hunts mice
and small animals. The big cats hunt deer
and large animals.

A cat often hunts at night.
He can see very well in dim light
and his whiskers help him
feel his way.

A cat has powerful jaws and sharp teeth
that bite and hold its prey.

A cat has five claws on each front paw, and four on each back paw. Most of the time the claws are hidden. But when a cat spreads its toes, the claws spring out.

A cat sits very still, watching its prey.
Then, it chases it and leaps on it.

Some big cats can run extremely fast.
The cheetah can go 60 miles an hour in a
burst of speed.

Between hunting trips, cats sleep a lot.
The mighty lion sometimes sleeps 19 hours a day.

If you have a cat, you've probably noticed it taking "cat naps" in the sun.

The first cats lived about 40 million years ago.
The most famous cat of the past was
the saber-toothed tiger, or Smilodon.

At different times in the past, people have believed that the mysterious cat was a god or a demon. Ancient Egyptians worshiped Bast, a goddess with a cat's head. They even made mummies of their dead cats.

In the Middle Ages,
some people believed
cats were demons
who helped witches.

Good luck or bad luck?
Even today, there is a superstition
—a silly belief—
that a black cat crossing your path
brings bad luck.
But in England, it's a
white cat that's supposed to
bring bad luck!

There are many different breeds of cats.

SIAMESE

PERSIAN

In a cat show, you can see the beauty
of such various breeds as Siamese, Persian,
Rex, and Russian Blue.

REX

RUSSIAN BLUE

One well-known breed
is the Siamese. These cats have
bright blue eyes and
dark marks or "points."

Another famous breed is the Persian.
These cats have long, silky fur.

The Manx is a peculiar cat—it has no tail.

Burmese cats have deep brown fur and golden eyes.

Some people think that Abyssinian
cats came from Egyptian cats.
They look like alley cats,
except that their fur is marked
like rabbit fur.

Rex cats are a newer breed.
They have a very soft, short, curly coat.

The Russian Blue cat is very rare.
Its coat is thick and has a blue-gray color
with a silvery sheen.

There are also thousands of mixed breed cats that are favorite family pets. They are also exhibited at cat shows along with the fancy breeds. Many mixed breed cats have won high honors for their beauty.

If you wanted a pet cat, which would you get?
It doesn't matter whether a cat is a purebred
or a mixed breed. Any cat will make a good pet
if you take care of it
and show it lots of love.

It is important to get a kitten that is the right age.
Two to four months is best.

Look for a lively kitten
which has clear eyes
and nice fur.

At first, feed the kitten twice a day.
When it is six months old, feed it once a day.
Make sure it always has fresh water.
Show a new kitten its bathroom—
the litter box. Change the litter
every few days.

Have your kitten examined and make sure it gets its shots.

You can pet your kitten so that it purrs...
and play exciting games with it.

Kittens are very playful and curious.

A cat is easy to care for.
It keeps itself clean
by washing its fur
with its rough tongue.

Perhaps a cat you know will have kittens. The babies grow for nine weeks before they are born.

When they are born, the mother licks them with her rough tongue
to clean them and to start their breathing.

Their eyes are shut, their ears are just tiny flaps, and they cannot smell very well. They know where the mother is because they can feel her purring.

When they are about five weeks old,
the kittens will be running and playing.

You can start feeding them
canned food or raw hamburger
from your fingertip. You can
also help them find
the litter box.

Kittens grow fast.
At eight or nine weeks,
they are ready to go to a new home.

Someday, maybe you will give
a new kitten to a friend.